Tim and Mariam

All the best for a happy and
adventurous 2019! Jon.

MW00748415

DARK WOOD

A Book of Poetry

Jon Ferry

Dark Wood Copyright © 2018 by Jon Ferry.

All rights reserved. No part of this book may be used or reproduced in any manner whatsoever without written permission except in the case of brief quotations embodied in critical articles or reviews.

Published by Prominence Publishing.
www.prominencepublishing.com

ISBN: 978-1-988925-27-1

First Edition: October 2018

Dedication

To those selfless souls who devote themselves to caring for others... who literally lay down their lives for their friends.

Table of Contents

Foreword

Robert Frost famously said a poem "begins in delight and ends in wisdom." And I think reading poems should be both a pleasure and an adventure. You should never quite know what you're getting into, but enjoy the ride nevertheless.

The breadth of poetry is amazing. It can be about a red wheelbarrow glazed with rainwater (William Carlos Williams) or about the kings and queens of England (Mary Ann H. T. Bigelow).

I like to write poems about beautiful things, such as elk and magnolia, or about personal things, such as death, loss and emotional turmoil. However, I don't shy away from controversial things, including the political and economic issues that threaten to disrupt our somewhat self-involved world.

Poetry really is a box of chocolates, with offerings that can be creamy and gooey or hard and nutty . . . and even stomach-churning. As Emily Dickinson said: "If I feel physically as if the top of my head were taken off, I know that is poetry."

For every high-flying poet that seems to abide by the so-called rules, there's one who ignores them so spectacularly you wonder what alien ship he or she just stepped down from. Or as Christopher Morley noted: "The courage of the poet is to keep ajar the door that leads into madness."

Poetry is an open door. And those who fancy themselves to be its gatekeepers -- who lecture others about what it should or shouldn't be -- tend to be either sourpuss moralists or control freaks.

In the meantime, all I can hope for is that this, my second book of poems, will give you some nuggets to feast on . . . without setting your teeth on edge.

Jon Ferry
North Vancouver, BC
September 2018

Dark Wood

In the middle of my life's journey,

I find myself in a dense, dark wood.

It's as poet Dante described it 700 years ago

when he was in a rather dour mood.

In his Divine Comedy, Dante journeyed

into hell to detail his abhorrence

of the vile political divisions that drove him

to say goodbye to his native Florence.

He described exile as having to leave

everything that he loved most . . . damned

to being a perpetual stranger and barred

from the home where he'd slept like a lamb.

My dark wood is wholly of my choosing.

I left my UK homeland of my own free will

when half the citizens there seemed on strike . . .

and life in North America seemed pretty chill.

I am an immigrant, not an exile.

Yet, I still pine for my native home . . .

and still miss many aspects of British life,

from bitter beer to the local building stone.

But I'm also mindful the world's population

is fast mutating into a multi-cultural sprawl,

with migrants streaming across porous borders

as if they'd never heard of the Berlin Wall.

Homo sapiens has been on the move for eons,

yearning to breathe freely from fresh oxygen.

As for tribal politics, there's little to distinguish

medieval Florence from swamp-like Washington.

Child Vision

A North African woman with a headscarf,
cradling a baby in her arms,
peers out over the Mediterranean
to Europe and its supposed charms.

Like other Third World migrants beating
down the doors of First World nations,
she's fixated on the hope of a better life
for herself, her child and future generations.

She also knows scores of asylum-seekers
never make it through the cruel maze.
Thousands more are killed, raped,
tortured and abused in other ways.

A North American woman, meanwhile,
leaves a clinic near the Golden Gate Bridge,
looking as if she's just visited a yoga studio
and is pleased with the outcome of her pledge.

Like other passionate "anti-natalists,"

this woman has had herself sterilized

because she believes burdening the planet

with another being is, well, uncivilized.

She's proud she's withstood the pressures

driving other young women to give birth

without fully appreciating the impact

on our exhausted, eco-ravaged Earth.

Two determined women, two different worlds.

One door open, the other closed.

One yearning for a brighter future,

the other doubting there's a future to unfold.

Wedding

Pack up the hats and the over-the-top dresses.

Dismantle the moon and the bright white sun.

The wedding's over. The hangover's just begun.

Brexit-weary Brits know how to throw a party,

out-dazzling Hollywood with sizzle and sparkle

and the genial grace of Givenchy-clad Markle.

Party-hearty Harry is our Prince Charming,

channeling Diana and doing his level best

to be Meghan's North, South, East and West.

The heroes of the hour are a gospel choir

and a U.S. bishop cooing like a dove

about the redeeming power of love.

We pray this fairy tale will never vanish,

And join the little girl asking in sorrow:

"Mummy, can we do it all again tomorrow?"

Well, can we make the dream last forever?

Can we ditch the rage and victimhood?

Or is nothing ever going to come to any good?

Black Panther

A watercourse on the way to paradise
is unlike most other worldly streams.
It glints with the sheen of a million nuggets,
and is named The River of Golden Dreams.

A mellow fellow is floating down the river
on a rudderless raft bloated with air.
He soon winds up in currents so vicious
he doesn't seem to have a hope or a prayer.

As he gets sucked into that boiling eddy,
the bubbling water starts to enter his lungs.
He's a hair's breadth away from drowning
when at long last his savior comes

in the form of a sleek black panther
patrolling lithely along the riverside.
The cat thrusts his paw into the whirlpool,
scooping up the man before he dies.

From then on in, the floater keeps sailing

along the gold-flecked stream of life.

But he's acutely aware a dream without a focus

is like a weekend warrior without a knife.

Lava Lover

Blow like a volcano.
Grow like a lily.
You go with the flow.
I scream shrilly.

Some explode out of the blocks.
Others start real slow,
steadily gaining steam
until they hit their plateau.

Some have a slow-burning fuse.
Others fire up like a Hemi,
rocketing down the track
as if they'd just won an Emmy.

Some see love as a Roman candle.
Others view it as a sparkler
lighting up the night sky,
then coolly turning darker.

Some run like a March hare.
Others dawdle like a tortoise.
They either opt for the easy hit
or choose to remain scoreless.

Some have a short attention span.
Others hold a long-term opinion.
They either channel testy Trump
Or mimic slick willy Clinton.

Some stew on a low heat.
Others bake on a high . . .
though temperature alone won't
guarantee them a piece of the pie.

Some select mates who look serious.
Others pick those who live to laugh.
But who would you rather marry?
Just ask your better half.

Blow like a volcano.
Grow like a lily.
You go with the flow.
I scream shrilly.

Generation of Hate

So sexpot Jane Fonda, the Hanoi wonder,
has finally closed up shop down under.

The love generation's long past its sell-by date,
yielding grudgingly to our era of hate.

Echo boomers hate baby boomers.
Baby boomers hate snowflake juniors.

Eco-believers hate climate deniers.
Eco-skeptics hate pretty little liars.

MeToo females hate mansplaining men.
Me-first males hate victim-playing women.

Whites hate the patter of Black Lives Matter.
Blacks hate white lies and other glib chatter.

Urbanites hate those pro-gun stickers.
Rural folks hate them big-city slickers.

Bicyclists hate gas-guzzling drivers.

Drivers hate road-hogging cyclers.

Fox News hates liberals lolling in the swamp.

CNN hates deplorables stomping for Trump.

Mainstream media hate fake web news.

Internet trolls hate lamestream views.

Freedom of speech has been turned on its ear.

Social justice warriors are starting to cheer.

Hanoi Jane is 80 and has shut up shop.

Everybody's hating each other nonstop.

Pork Farm

Slice, dice, slice, dice.
We're cutting into the ham –
the hind leg of the porker
or a solid chunk of spam.

Ours is a slice-and-dice society,
divided into racial groups,
carved into ethnic bands,
ground into gender troupes.

Slice, dice, dice, slice.
We're cutting into the ham –
the hind leg of the porker
or a solid chunk of spam.

It's no longer we the people
who together answer the call
to secure the blessings of liberty
for the betterment of all.

Slice, dice, slice, dice.
We're cutting into the ham –
the hind leg of the porker
or a solid chunk of spam.

All animals are equal on this farm,
save those more equal than others.
Now, all you need is victim status
to help you hose your brothers.

Slice, dice, dice, slice.
We're cutting into the ham –
the hind leg of the porker
or a solid chunk of spam.

It's not what you know or do,
but the color of your hide
that wins you the social license
to wallow in the mudslide.

Slice, dice, slice, dice.
We're cutting into the ham –
the hind leg of the porker
or a solid chunk of spam.

To be a "working person,"
you don't have to work,
simply squeak like a piglet
and curse like a total jerk.

Slice, dice, dice, slice.
We're cutting into the ham –
the hind leg of the porker
or a solid chunk of spam.

Being "middle class" used to be OK,
until the boars aped Robin Hood
to rob you of what you earned
and gouge you for your own good.

Slice, dice, slice, dice.
We're cutting into the ham –
the hind leg of the porker
or a solid chunk of spam

So are you dazed and confused?
Well, switching your sexual identity
provides enticing options
for massaging your celebrity.

Slice, dice, dice, slice.
We're cutting into the ham –
the hind leg of the porker
or a solid chunk of spam.

In a slice-and-dice-society,
the worst identity is being old.
So grab your seniors' pass,
your views smell like mold.

Slice, dice, slice, dice.
We're cutting into the ham –
the hind leg of the porker
or a solid chunk of spam.

There's no space for individual thought
in our diversity-obsessed world.
Just wave your tribal flag aloft
and grunt like the rest of the herd.

Mountain Tennis

There's a tennis court that I know,

high among Canada's wild Coast Mountains.

It reminds me of what my father said

about how life has few absolutes,

just shifting contrasts and abrupt surprises.

Tennis courts were once suburban structures

peopled by accountants and other upper-crust

men in shorts and tasteful tennis shoes...

and willowy women with pretty white dresses,

colored headbands and elegant backhands.

They featured restrained clatter, muted chatter,

gentle clapping, discreet smiling

and modest primping and preening...

topped off perhaps with strawberries and cream

of the kind so beloved at Wimbledon.

But on this owl-friendly ridge among the crags
of British Columbia, not too far from Whistler
or the steam-belching volcano of Mount Meager,
all you hear is the distant rumble of the odd
mudslide, boulder slide... or avalanche.

It's grizzly-bear country, interrupted
only by a subdivision of lone-wolf homes
that appear as if they might be a little lost...
or at least could be more artfully arranged
in a more compact neighborhood.

Tennis is a dynamite sport for stretching
tense backs, tight thighs and wrinkled faces.
It's ideal for refreshing the heart and lungs
and boosting focus and relaxation...
not to mention the opportunity for mixed doubles.

And in this sweet spot, just below a log cabin,
a manicured tennis court makes a bold statement
about humans' unrelenting drive for civilization.
The reason, though, it punches way above its weight
are the snowy skyscrapers towering majestically over it.

Cruelest Game

I don't get too much sleep these days.
I'm far too busy viewing
the World Cup of soccer
on my flickering television.

And I can't count the myriad of ways
that watching tattooed millionaires
chase after a bladder-filled ball
interferes with my mental vision.

Prolonged periods of broken plays
followed by intense surges
of pure pandemonium
unhinge the heart's soothing rhythm.

Each grueling tournament phase
compounds the hysteria
of those who've turned a kids' game
into a metaphor for a war mission.

Ronaldo, Messi, Neymar and Suarez

are the heroes the critics like best.

But even they get ripped to shreds

for some luckless glitch or indecision.

The Beautiful Game is a fine-sounding phrase

that can't hope to describe the lottery

in which winners are feted like gods

and losers damned to eternal perdition.

Don't believe what the baying mob says.

Soccer is the cruelest game...

where a rush of blood to the head

destroys the first flush of enthusiasm.

Blowtorch Blowback

We all have our fair share of fine intentions,
but so often they result in misapprehensions.
We rush to the aid of a driver on the road,
only for him to turn around and rob us cold.

Ontario politicians bent on curbing fossil fuels
seemed shocked when their new green rules
helped cause electricity bills there to soar,
burning both city dwellers and the rural poor.

One of the worst stories, though, I have heard
about worthy aspirations becoming blurred
is that of a Tucson man who had the lofty goal
of killing the spiders under his mobile home.

The blowtorch he used to zap the critters
that were giving the family the jitters
started a blaze, which engulfed the trailer.
It gutted the house like a drunken sailor.

As British author Aldous Huxley mentions,

the road to hell isn't just paved with good intentions.

It's walled, roofed and furnished with a potpourri

of duplicity, hypocrisy and stupidity.

Humpty Dumpty

Whenever you drop a key, ball or chocolate egg,

it invariably lands a long way from where

you think it should, eventually settling in

under the bed, couch . . . or otherwise managing

to find a cranny where it can bury its head.

The object goes where it's determined to be,

out of your narrow, dwindling sight,

beyond your shrinking, limited reach,

free from your officer-like command . . .

like a stubborn, escape-hungry fly or flea.

It's the same when your kindest, closest mates

suddenly up and leave for a faraway place.

They remain good eggs, but over time

the distance between you becomes so stretched

it reaches the point the relationship breaks.

My wife and I had a couple of great friends

when our son and their daughter were growing up.

Hardly a day went by when we didn't chat to them ...

at least until they found a new life in another town

and we started viewing each other through a different lens.

Instead of talking for comfort and mutual pleasure,

we got all hung up on petty arrangements,

such as the days of the week we could phone

or the weeks we could or couldn't visit.

It's no wonder we wound up shunning each other.

Years later, we tried to pick up where we'd left off.

We found a sliver of the old connection was there,

but the times had changed. So had our politics.

We got on our high horse about everything

from extreme climate change to Anton Chekhov.

A busted friendship is like an inkless pen

or a shattered piece of fine bone china.

You just have to keep reminding yourself

that all the king's horses and all the king's men

couldn't put Humpty Dumpty together again.

Blackberries

Blackberries shouldn't be picked, they say,
after October 11, Old Michaelmas Day.
I understand why that's the case;
they go from ripe to rotten to taste.

The world of politics is changing fast.
Toxic offshoots from our troubled past
threaten yet again to add deadly stress
to years of mellow fruitfulness.

The world is perched precariously
between warring ideologies.
The threat of nuclear war hangs over all
from clown dictator Kim Jong-un.

Our collective memories are short
about the destruction that was wrought
during the Depression and two world wars,
all for some plausible-sounding cause.

A gathering storm in the West,
now manifests itself in petrol-bomb protest.
The sharp divide between rich and poor
is code for evening up the score.

A rise in nationalism and populism
confronts a resurgence in communism.
Ethnic hatred fuels the combination
of brutish terrorism and bully-boy migration.

Political correctness has choked our will
to be frank about the collective skill
needed to balance competing alternatives
and curb the spread of raging furnaces.

After summer and before Santa Claus,
fall is the season in which we pause
to cool dangerously high fevers
and rein in egotistical leaders.

Picking blackberries is a sharp reminder
of the fruit Mother Nature can provide us –
and how swiftly it can all wither,
if we continue to bicker and dither.

No Escape

You could say I'm a travelin' man.
I hate sitting still and staying put,
infinitely preferring life in a Kombi van
to knowing where I'll put my next foot.

I'm a dyed-in-the-wool hippie,
who fancies the kiss of the wind in his hair,
and whether in Wyoming or Mississippi
always dreams of castles in the air.

Some are wont to call me a gypsy,
with a fondness for fortune-telling.
Others feel I have a weakness for getting tipsy,
especially with women who are compelling.

Most think I'm a diehard drifter,
with no compass or direction --
or at least a chronic shape-shifter,
constantly changing form and complexion.

I am a man of no fixed abode,
with no firm conviction or belief
and no will to pull over to the side of the road
while being blown around like a falling leaf.

Call me a migrant or a vagrant,
I have no particular goal or ambition.
I may be a long-term benefits claimant,
but I am certainly no homing pigeon.

But what I have learned on this planet,
whether motionless or on the move,
is that it's easy to adopt a habit
and get sucked into a rut-filled groove.

That's why half-way through your life
you generally wind up prisoner to a pattern
laid down by a controlling wife
or mapped out by the local tavern.

The furrows etched on your face,
the lines that make you look tense
show you cannot change life's pace.
Travel won't make any difference.

You are the captain of your ship.

You are the creator of your health.

Taking off from the nearest airstrip

will not help you escape yourself.

Opinions

The world's big problem, my mother-in-law says,

is that everybody's got an opinion.

She's absolutely right, of course.

Opinions now have dominion.

They get into scrapes and ugly debates,

causing multiple headaches.

And despite their tiresome japes,

they still sizzle like hot cakes.

They keep popping up on social media

where everyone's irate

and the way to get media attention

is to peddle venom and hate.

Others have other opinions about opinions.

They praise them for voicing concerns

about everything from climate change

to social justice and gender pronouns.

They claim that a world without opinions
is like battered fish without chips
or steak without onions...
or a pit bull without a leash.

My mother-in-law grew up in an era when
journalists strove to report the truth,
not fake news and other propaganda...
and when "science" was based on proof.

She also went to posh dinner parties
where being tipsy was no crime.
But if you spewed strident opinions,
you were viewed as a bit of a slime.

Being branded opinionated, in fact,
was as bad as being caught naked.
It stripped you of your modesty
and made you seem degraded.

The opinions, though, we all still like
are those that mirror our own.
And those of mine others like most
are those that I've never shown.

Sacrifice

Greater love hath no woman
than that she lays down her life
for a child, a parent or a friend.

Greater comfort hath no woman
than in finding a friend
on whom she can truly depend.

Greater joy hath no woman
than in producing a child
they labor together to tend.

Greater satisfaction hath no woman
than in raising that child
with an ardor that cannot be stemmed.

Greater anguish hath no woman
than in losing her mate to an
addiction she can't comprehend.

Greater sorrow hath no woman
than in watching their child
go inexorably round the bend.

Greater hardship hath no woman
than in keeping an aging parent
alive until the bitter end.

Greater challenge hath no woman
than in fixing a broken family
that's almost impossible to mend.

Greater love hath no woman
than that she sacrifices her life
for what she struggles to defend.

Christmas Lights

Go big or go home might well have been the motto
of the palatial house with its Christmas lights
illuminating the water-view street like a grotto
bathed in a million laser-like delights.

Zipped together in electric latticework,
hundreds of feet of timed LED bulbs
launched a flood of colors going berserk
in and around the mansion's garden shrubs.

We pulled our auto over onto the gravel.
Then, drenched in light, we began to disembark
amidst all the kaleidoscopic razzle-dazzle
of a packed Walt Disney theme park.

Other motorists were doing exactly the same.
And the street of our dreams became jammed
with gawkers equally eager to lay claim
to the Yuletide cheer cleverly programmed.

So we left and headed on up two blocks

to a nondescript street far less glitzy and rich

in mind-blowing tones and psychedelic lighting props...

and far more prone to using a dimmer switch.

My top prize, in fact, for the most graceful

lights were the low-tech ones loosely strewn

over a squat Japanese split-leaf maple.

They were little red flags on a lost saloon.

No computer gimmickry was propelling them.

They simply gleamed like those that glowed

in and around a lowly stable in Bethlehem...

where the light of the world emerged so long ago.

Mighty Magnolia

Of all Earth's flowering shrubs,

the one I love the most

is the magnificent magnolia.

Its white, pink and purple

blossoms are the clearest

sign that spring is here.

Magnolia blooms take many forms,

from a lotus-shaped goblet

to a dainty, finger-like star.

They're the official flower

of everywhere from Louisiana

and Mississippi to North Korea.

But don't be too hasty

to judge this chart-topping book

by its charming southern cover.

These ancient trees are as tough
as movieland's steel magnolias
and can survive much longer.

Fossil records suggest magnolias
have been around for the last
hundred million years.

Bold and lush, they light up
our grey world with a blast of color...
without guilt, without fear.

Rabbit in Winter

Little rabbit by the road,
huddled up against the cold.

Little rabbit's twitching nose
sniffs for predatory crows.

Little rabbit makes me smile,
dreaming of Easter in a while,

with little rabbit haring around
the daffodil-dotted ground.

Little rabbit so vulnerable,
like a baby in a stable.

Little rabbit, Peter Rabbit,
children's joy, parents' panic.

Walking Away

It may not have been meant to be that way,

here in this sunny hayfield flanked by cottonwoods,

staring up at the brilliance of the big mountain,

squinting at the other snowy peaks on display.

It may have been the stifling, late-spring heat

and the fatiguing onset of crippling hay fever.

But there I was, bent over like a sack of potatoes,

with mucus streaming from my beak.

It could be that Gaia, goddess of nature,

was acting like any self-respecting neighbor,

unable to accept that some out-of-town drifter

would seek to possess heaven's half acre.

Or perhaps I'd found a unique way to record

that, out of acute fear of missing out,

I was buckling under heavy realtor pressure

to purchase a parcel of land I could ill afford.

What I do know is I limped off that village lot,

with my reddened eyes itching furiously

and my face discolored and contorted,

like the limp victim of a twisted garrote.

My only comfort was a lesson well learned

that, when pursuing a prized property,

walking away is often sound policy. And traveling light

is usually the best way to view the world.

Jump Start

Tired of the same old, same old?

Bored with getting stuck in the mud?

Take the road far less traveled

and rid yourself of the crud.

Struggling with a midlife crisis?

Sick of being moody and morose?

Waking up happy is priceless.

So go out and chase your goals.

Fatigued by fixed opinions?

Alarmed by the rigid clock?

Blow away ho-hum decisions

and rocket from the starting block.

Frayed by feeling lethargic?

Rattled by the lump in your throat?

Seek out a climb that's cathartic

and scale it like a mountain goat.

Fed up with lacking stamina?

Drained by the latest dead-end?

Ditch your selfie-taking camera.

Leap into life's saddle again.

Bent over by beating the old drum?

Burned out by swigging stale hype?

If you don't like what you've become...

well, try becoming what you like.

Medicine Man

The mountain towers 7,000 feet over the valley,

with the sheerest of icy gullies for veins --

and a shape that reminds neighboring natives

of an old medicine man with vision and brains.

The man was a great hunter in his prime.

But he later learned to read signs from space

and to predict local weather changes by how

the clouds ducked below the mountain's face.

He employed the power of medicinal plants

to cure domestic dysfunction and repression.

He had an unerring feel for signals of

mental ill health and deadly depression.

The sole remaining task in his eventful life

was to secure the well-being of his native band

by appointing a vigorous successor

to perform the vital duties under his command.

His two brash sons were bold and strong.

They were passionate and enthusiastic.

But they feuded so much with each other

he wondered if either was a suitable candidate.

To test their mettle, he decided to give them a trial

high in the mountain -- beside where a raging falls

had helped carve a dizzying gap between

the narrowest of remote canyon walls.

Jumping this gap would bring them fame.

Failure to do so could mean instant death.

Yet, their father felt they needed a leap of faith

to earn them some sorely needed tribal respect.

The elder son failed to make it fully across,

falling onto a fir whose limbs started bending.

His arms screamed with pain, his iron will ebbed

and he warned his sibling against trying to save him.

The younger son asked his dad whether he should
seize his own chance to be a great leader –
or help his brother, at great risk to himself,
avoid the fate for which he was clearly so eager.

His stern father left it for him to decide.
So, ignoring his older brother, he made the jump,
cheating oblivion by clinging to the opposing wall
and hauling himself up clump by clump.

The dad, meanwhile, set about saving his older son,
throwing a lasso over him with expert precision.
He dragged him back up across the abyss,
bruised, bloodied and barely breathing.

The medicine man then yelled at his other son:
"You may be game, but you lack an inner guide.
I need someone less self-centred than you
to take responsibility for this ornery tribe."

For months before their illustrious father died,

the brothers still bickered and battled violently.

But when they traversed the peak's near-vertical slopes,

they ensured they calmed down, moving silently.

Tribal elders say that later, while out goat-hunting,

the pair were struck by lightning and turned to stone.

But their chiseled faces still stare out from the mountain...

and their father's proud spirit still calls them home.

Ghost Rider

I see you at lunchtime
or during dinner,
loping rhythmically
down by the river.

I see you at breakfast
or during happy hour,
jumping the fence
beside the watchtower.

I see you at nighttime
in my dreams,
galloping with the stars
until daylight intervenes.

I see you in the mirror
behind my back,
as the rain washes down
our garden shack.

I see you on the beach
below the white clover,
tasting the sea spray,
heroic like Homer.

I see your beloved horse,
rearing in fear,
your torso twisted
under its rear.

I see you on the ground,
staring up at the sun,
your body broken,
your day done.

I see you on the hillside,
running free,
heading to greener pastures
for all eternity.

I see you in my head.
I feel you in my heart.
I will always be with you.
We will never be apart.

Sacred and Profane

A haiku

Pilgrims in April

trip round the love pole in May.

They dance, ride and pray.

Christmas Bubbles

With its soaring highs and brutal lows,

Christmas can be a crushingly cruel

time of year, especially for those

who believe they have to do it all.

So I went to the local waterfront market

to spread around some Yuletide cheer,

only to find the outside temperature

matched the frostiness of shoppers there.

Even the salespeople didn't seem

too interested in what I had in my pocket.

It took all my charm to persuade a store clerk

to help me buy my son a wallet.

And down by the pilings where the ferry docks,

the fat gulls and sleek cormorants

appeared curiously disinclined

to dip their beaks into the currents.

They were too busy either squawking
to each other or drinking in the silhouette
of downtown skyscrapers across the water,
basking in the winter sun's caress.

My eye was drawn to a young mom
calmly pushing a pram on the wharf,
accompanied by two happy little girls,
one with a pink, the other with a purple scarf.

Moments later, I was walking between
the soap bubbles that they had blown,
feeling as if I was floating on air
in a freshly-painted Impressionist zone.

A load was lifted off my shoulders,
knowing all it took to restore Christmas
was the magic of translucent little pockets
of simple joy . . . and childlike crispness.

Snow

Snow is a lot like love.
You either have way too much of it
or not nearly enough.

It's a devoted pal
who hangs around for far too long
or doesn't stay at all.

And when it first shows up,
it's a crispy-crunchy miracle.
Then, it quickly turns to slush.

But a world without snow
is like a cake without icing
or a bride without her beau.

Snow garnishes the trees
with a thick coat of whipping cream.
It lets us breathe and release.

It makes our world cozier,

sweeter, fresher and, above all, slower.

It snuffs out the mediocre.

It tells our absurdly rushed,

entitled, egotistical universe

to listen for once and be hushed.

The best part of snow, though,

is when it comes and when it goes,

touching us more deeply than we know.

High Life

My grandfather was a mountain man.
He far preferred an ugly crampon
to any buried hoard of treasure
or brass sculpture by Auguste Rodin.

I, too, have my mountain moments
when I inhale the fine air and azure sky
and gaze at layers of snow-clad spires,
their glinting sides invitingly frozen.

I can't say, though, I have much interest
in slogging my own way up those slopes.
I'd rather leave that to a willing horse
or other sturdy vehicle I can trust.

Lowly valleys don't ring my bell either,
especially those that are prone to flooding.
One of my worst nightmares involves
a soggy basement becoming wetter.

But if between the two I had to pick a winner,

I'd choose mountain over valley living every time.

Being able to view the tense world below

offers a riveting reason not to gripe or bicker.

Yes, my grandpa was an alpine master;

he made sure mountains were in my genes.

Seeing them stand tall like noble sculptures

relaxes me . . . and makes my heart beat faster.

Sounds of Kindness

There's little more magical
than a bugling elk ghosting its way
through a mountain meadow
on a crisp, early fall day.

There's little more wonderful
than the neighing of an Arab stallion
in the desert heat, snorting like
a trumpeter heading a battalion.

There's little more beautiful
than the sound of surf in motion
on a white, oatmeal-sand beach
beside the turquoise ocean.

There's little more soulful
than an old country steeple
with its bells in full spring swing,
calling you to pray with the people.

Nothing, though, is more meaningful

than a true friend's consoling words

trilling through your soul . . .

like a symphony of songbirds.

Sun God

I'm at an age when I don't have

much faith in gods any more.

But if I had to pick one,

it'd be the sun god... or goddess.

I'd worship this god in the early spring

when the sun's playfully battling

puffy clouds and a gentle wind

to finally bring the world some bling.

I'd pray for its spectacular, mushrooming light

to radiate softly through my being,

dispelling the rigid ferocity

of Boreas, the Greek god of winter.

Some experts say that we have to protect

ourselves from solar damage

with shiny Aviator glasses like

cool cops wear in bone-dry places.

Others say the heat of the sun is now

so extreme through climate change

and runaway greenhouse warming

our planet will soon be as parched as Venus.

But here on North America's frigid Wet Coast,

the sun remains a beguiling heater,

an inviting beacon in a squally sea,

a spreader of harmony, not arid intensity.

Here, the morning sunlight is no skin-shriveling,

sweat-inducing exhaustion driver.

It's a Vitamin D provider,

mood-enhancing healer and stress reliever.

And on a bright spring day, there's nothing finer

than squinting out with your scrawny neck

at its glinting rays dancing on water.

The sun god is glowing... hope is on deck.

Life Sport

Life is a lot like sport.

You play to win,

not simply occupy the court.

Life is like soccer.

It's a beautiful game

played by your average plodder.

Life is like cricket.

The pitch is parched

or it's a pretty sticky wicket.

Life is like baseball.

You have nine innings

to make no headway at all.

Life is like tennis.

Lose games to love,

and you're in a tricky crevice.

Life is like ice hockey.

Shoot some, brawl some,

and everybody gets cocky.

Life is like juggling.

Let one ball fall,

and you're really struggling.

Like is like snooker.

Make a bad break,

and it's a pressure cooker.

Life is like horse-racing.

The odds are ugly . . .

but you have to keep chasing.

Choices

Dropped into the bar the other day,

drinking too much as usual,

when the female server asked

why I looked so mournful.

Said I once had a smiley face

as a rancher striving to get ahead.

But all that changed when I caught

a burglar rifling through my toolshed.

Told her how I grabbed my gun,

aimed it at the man's chest.

Ordered him to remain still

or I'd put him permanently to rest.

Punk chose to ignore my bluster,

cursing and slamming the door.

Chased after him, heart thumping,

sweating from every pore.

Fired off a couple of warning rounds

as he loped along the levee

to join his hopped-up buddies

hooting and hollering in their SUV.

Double-locked everything that night,

in case those gangbangers returned

with firepower of their own

and I wound up getting burned.

Sheriff showed up next morning,

grilled me about an Indian youth

who'd taken a bullet in his thigh

that caused him to bleed out.

Told the lawman this was simply

a sorry chapter in a sick saga.

We landowners were bone weary

of home invasions and other drama.

Said I regretted the decision I made,

but so should those young men

who crisscrossed the prairie,

stealing stuff, causing mayhem.

Neighboring ranchers cheered my stand.

Native leaders called me a racist ogre.

I reminded the judge I was just

protecting myself from a trespasser.

All-white jury let me beat the rap.

Yet, the outcry over the non-sentence

led to my selling the farm

and moving away for my penance.

So there I was inviting the server

to continue our barroom discussions

about the "accident" that destroyed one man,

fueling racial repercussions.

Abruptly, her face went beet red.

Said she knew all about the case.

It was her cousin that I'd killed,

and he was far from a waste of space.

Stay away from here, she hissed,

you and your white man's slander.

I know by the mark of Cain on your face

you'll always be a restless wanderer.

Moral of this story is we all

make choices, and some go haywire.

But the most terrible occur when

we play judge, jury... and executioner.

Independence

Catalonia wants to set up its own nation.
Scotland seems to want to do so, too.
From Quebec to Venice and Sardinia,
folks are bent on so-called self-rule.

But these heritage-hungry separatists
alarm leaders of western democracies
now busy turning once-tribal cities
into multi-ethnic bureaucracies.

The nationalists say multiculturalism
ghettoizes countries, tearing them asunder,
and that mass immigration and racial strife
go together like lightning and thunder.

They question why our governments keep
importing queue-jumpers and other people
from countries with values and beliefs
that appear frighteningly medieval.

They believe an ethnically-divided country
without some compelling reason
for its collective national existence
all too quickly loses its cohesion.

They ask why we don't make it easier
for couples that are homegrown
to get better jobs and more schooling ...
and produce more children of their own.

But liberal politicians and professors
counter that immigration is the only way
to boost declining population levels
and save the economy from decay.

Universities teach impressionable students
that racial and gender diversity
is one of the paramount virtues
society must pursue with raw intensity.

Pundits note America was built on immigration

and has always been a melting pot.

They argue the best way for diverse cultures

to end war is to love each other a lot.

But what they themselves clearly detest

is diversity of thought and opinion

on everything from racial quotas

to gender selection and Hillary Clinton.

They want the great unwashed to have

a single, unchallengeable world view

that lumps chicken curries and fortune cookies

into one giant, multi-ethnic stew.

I say great minds may think alike,

but that fools seldom differ.

Sure, we should keep an open mind.

Yet, we shouldn't sell ourselves down the river.

Home Bells

Out walking today, a nerve in my shin is acting up.

I'm twitching fitfully, thinking about the things

I have and haven't done here over the years --

five thousand miles from the old British house

where I once heard the church bells ring.

The trail meanders along the seaside woods

down to the boathouse in the cove.

It runs through the park I'd take dear Toby,

our muscular mastiff-pointer cross,

to let him bulldoze the undergrowth.

But this crisp fall day, it's my mind that wanders.

Momentarily, I become disoriented,

scrambling in the midst of a tangled thicket,

powering past towering evergreens,

searching for where I first went adrift.

Grunting and grabbing, sliding and slipping,

I'm frantic to solve the riddle of the forest maze --

when, like an old friend, the trail emerges to greet

and guide me alongside mammoth rocks

to drink in the last of the sinking sun's rays.

My leg pain has gone now. But if the truth be told,

I was never too worried about going off the rails.

I knew, in the end, I'd find a way back

to the closest thing to a home I'd ever known.

I even sensed, for a second, the sound of bells.

Inspiration

It's something we need as a way
to stir the brain's chemistry
and raise our gut's ability
to hoist heavy arms and legs
out of bed on a low-energy day.

It's something tradespeople know,
however uncertain their jobs,
that what their freezing mitts do
builds a nest egg for their families
and boosts the wealth of the globe.

It's something entrepreneurs feast on,
that gives them the will to invest in
their wildly disruptive dream
of domestic business success
or world financial domination.

It's something reporters use as fuel
to continue pursuing the truth,
chasing windmills, puncturing balloons,
however often it's a dead end
that turns into cold, thin gruel.

It's something that poets crave,
the delicious juxtaposition of ideas,
the tension of smoldering desire,
the faint tug of stationary objects,
the yearning for a long-lost cave.

It's something for the lack of which
we turn into hollow creatures
with feelings like wooden boards . . .
and potentially uplifting thoughts
mashed into a single bland dish.

Aspiration drives us towards our goals.
But inspiration is how God created
humans from the ground's dirt,
breathing spirit into their nostrils,
transforming them into living souls.

Conversation High

There is nothing finer in this world

than the congenial art of conversation.

It sets up virtually everything else

that merits human consideration.

You can have all the latest gadgets

and perkiest robots at your command.

But if you can't talk face to face to others,

you'll never be that much in demand.

You may be the world's most powerful figure

with a flotilla of Ferraris in your garage.

Yet if you aren't skilled at verbal ping pong,

life simply becomes an empty mirage.

William Hazlitt said the essence of conversation

is that of hearing as well as being heard.

Guy de Maupassant called conversation a mystery

consisting of the art of never seeming bored.

No one thinks conversation is always easy.

Indeed, the Marquis de Sade intimated

that, like certain portions of the anatomy,

it runs more smoothly when lubricated.

One thing I've figured out is that conversation

often comes in fits, spurts and starts.

So if you're ready to look, learn and listen,

you'll snag your fair share of hearts.

Pundits say folks now are so busy texting

they no longer need to look people in the eye.

But humans are not solitary creatures;

they can't fake intimacy to get a real high.

Memories

The most wonderful thing about life
is what we have been given for free --
our switched-on brain, for example,
with its massive storage capacity.

Our recollections flit in and out
of our heads like waves of wasps.
We go about our business, not knowing
when or where they may pop up.

Most common are those memories that
have been converted into corny floppies,
featuring you sunning on a beach in Hawaii
or me riding a cow pony in the Rockies.

Then, there are those dark flashbacks
that are far harder to assimilate,
of me scowling like a heavy cloud
or you in an equally unforgiving state.

But some memories sizzle with romance,

like when we bumped into each other in London.

You say my blue eyes attracted you;

I fixated on your passion for fashion.

The day you gave birth to our son,

you held him intently to your breast.

You both looked so interconnected,

so well-fitting, just like a snug vest.

But the reason, I think, we're still together,

despite being rather nervous and uptight,

is we share such magnetic memories.

Living apart would never ever feel right.

Wind of Change

Driving on a sunny fall day,
I hit a wind gust along the way.
Here and there it curled and twirled
like a great sail being unfurled.

The flurry became a tumble dryer,
turning my whole world haywire.
Golden leaves swirled like shiny coins;
green ones whirled like flakes on steroids.

I slowed my high-revving car awhile,
gripping the wheel, forcing a smile,
querying the source of the squall
that was answering nature's call.

My heart was thumping in my chest,
apprehensive about the next test
that autumn would fling in my path
as part of its abrupt fit of wrath.

I took in several deep breaths

to offset all that blustery excess...

when as quickly as it came, the breeze

tailed off into a hushed deep freeze.

I carried on gingerly down the road,

sensing this seasonal miracle was code

for a stormy year that's busy aging...

and a fractious globe that's fast changing.

Prayer

Why does one person remain poverty-stricken?

Why does another become a millionaire?

Why are men and women so different?

Why do opposites form a pair?

Why is living together so difficult?

Why is it so hard to share?

Why is owning a fancy home so crucial?

Why do we really care?

Why is choosing clothes such a worry?

Why stew over what we wear?

Why do some people seem so dull?

Why do others have such flair?

Why it so hard to keep old friends?

Why are good ones so rare?

Why are we so chronically anxious?

Why not simply avoid any scare?

Why are memories so important?

Why is living for now so bare?

Why do some of us die so early?

Why do others outlive their heir?

Why is life so hopelessly complicated?

Why is it so terribly unfair?

Why do we look beyond us for an answer?

Why do we resort to prayer?

Coming and Going

There is a trail I've come to know

that seems so very different,

depending on the way you go.

One way, to your right,

is a vintage farm and windmill

that looks like a heritage site.

From there, the gravel track rises

to a makeshift bench set

amidst bushes of various sizes.

It's a lookout that's ideal

for hopping off your bike

and contemplating your navel.

That way, your eye is directed

across a hayfield to where shapely

trees and homes are inter-connected.

Stacked above them like a picture,

snowy mountains divinely soar

two miles above the valley floor.

It may seem fanciful to assert

the meaning of life is contained

in some two-way stretch of dirt.

But coming or going on that footpath,

I've never ever had to wonder

whether it was worth the effort.

Lord of the Flies

I have something in my eye
that's giving me fake views.
I feel I'm being stalked by a fly
and otherwise abused.

They call these specks floaters
that cast shadows on our retinas.
But they act more like the rotors
of choppers hovering over us.

It's easy to become paranoid
when you're always monitored --
and to become antsy and annoyed
when your vision gets fogged.

Yet there's no dodging the fact
that we live in a sheer bubble
where we're forever tracked.
Breathing freely is a struggle.

The process starts with mothers
obsessed with vigilance.
Then come significant others
schooled in surveillance.

Banks monitor each transaction;
computers count every click.
Store cameras report each infraction;
vehicle data recorders every trick.

There's big money in big data.
Every action pads a brief
that can be sold to a retailer,
insurance firm or corporate thief.

We are a spy society.
We leave no one alone,
even as we amp up their anxiety
about the great unknown.

Big Brother's job is to scrutinize
rich and poor, short and tall...
to let the Lord of the Flies,
Beelzebub, rule over all.

Best Friends

So much depends upon the wedding
of Prince Harry and Meghan Markle.
In a world that's very heavy sledding,
we're desperate for some light sparkle.

So sparkle is what we've got... and passion
and Hollywood glory and royal good looks.
Meghan and Harry's fame is the height of fashion,
given her starring role in the hit series Suits.

It's a pairing that could be viewed as a bit odd,
with a biracial, California career woman
teaming up with a British blue blood
best known for his quenchless thirst for fun.

Harry's mom was a fairy princess and style icon;
Meghan's is a yoga instructor and social worker.
So theirs is simply Cinderella fan fiction
reworked for our identity-obsessed era.

And they'll need all that allure in force

for this union to stay true to its mission.

Some 40 per cent of U.S. marriages end in divorce,

a figure that isn't much better in Britain.

But let's get one thing perfectly straight:

initially, at any rate, people desire

the same sort of qualities in a mate

as they do, say, in a modern motor car.

They go for the lustrous paint, the upscale make

and the thrilling, high-performance engine.

But as they age, they opt for a less showy shape.

They settle for a vehicle of less pretension.

My humble opinion is that what Harry, Meghan

and all of us ought to be seeking in the end

is more durable than celebrity obsession.

We should plan to marry our best friend.

Sologamy

Dressed in a white gown,
the fitness trainer is joined
by friends and family,
and she seems overjoyed.

She has a honeymoon in Egypt
to look forward to, so we're told.
It's the icing on the cake
for the fairytale wedding to unfold.

But there's no groom in sight,
no ravishing Prince Charming.
This woman is marrying herself.
It's all rather disarming.

News reports suggest sologamy
has supplanted monogamy
for those who see shared toothbrushes
as the icons of marital monotony.

Self-love, not self-denial,

is now the glue that binds society.

There's no need to get married

to another to express your loyalty.

And if all you're seeking is a series

of steamy one-stand nights,

porn galore is a click away.

So are online dating sites.

As for population growth,

we in the western nations

can keep importing migrants

to boost family formations.

Sologamists are so like Liberace;

they're wedded to their vanity.

Their own self-worth means so much

more than everyone else's sanity.

Old Man and his Ravens

A pair of ravens circle the car park
two-thirds of the way up the dormant volcano,
waiting for an old man to dole out
food for them from an aluminum container.

The chatty ravens wheel from tree to tree,
then drop lightly onto the tarmac
where the man pulls strips of meat
from a tinfoil packet he carries in his knapsack.

The retired engineer first met the aerial acrobats
while picking blueberries five years ago
on this family-friendly North Vancouver ski hill.
He found them friendlier than any human he ran into.

But he has no real need now to make the
daily pilgrimage along the winding road from downtown.
Nor do the brazen ravens need him for nourishment;
there are goodies galore to scavenge on the mountain.

People used to refer to a "conspiracy of ravens."
Local natives, though, know they're not just tricksters.
They're agents of change, bringing critical
messages from a myriad of shape-shifters.

They clearly touch the deep, wild core
of this veteran, Ukrainian-born traveler.
He, meanwhile, brings out their domestic side,
their playful curiosity about human aroma.

The meal is over in seconds. And the ravens,
mates for life, don't hang around to bless him.
They don't have to. His leathery face is glowing.
At 92, he's still grinning, still giving, still growing.

Seagulls at Happy Hour

I swear I heard the word "hello"
as I took a break on the rocky beach,
drinking in the last of the Pacific sun
turning its fiery face into a glowing peach.

So I turned around to look for a friend,
though wondering what buddy of mine
would be outside braving the icy wind
when he could be inside with a glass of wine.

No mere human, however, had my back.
There was no instant flash of recognition,
just a few yapping dogs haring about,
oblivious to their owners' supervision.

I heard hello again and again,
before noticing the insistent greeting
was not from a pal, but from a pushy gull
seeking a partner for its genial tweeting.

Seagulls are not the most beautiful birds.

They're not celebrated in ancient tales

of courtly knights embracing falconry

or other pursuits where chivalry prevails.

They squabble, screech, scavenge and shriek.

But they're nothing if not zippy and vigorous.

They can walk, fly, swim, hover, couple

for life... and are shamelessly omnivorous.

Whether using the rocks to crack open shells

or stealing snacks from gullible beach-goers,

they're thrilled to show off their flying skills,

crane their necks or ripple their shoulders.

Their vulgar chatter, though, reminded me

we humans have our raucous moments, too.

At happy hour, we love to say hello

to our mates... and generally raise a hullabaloo.

Heavenly Bodies

As we age more or less stoically,

we increasingly yearn for a shot at immortality,

or at least something less perishable

than a bland name etched on a tired wall.

Anti-aging pills may soon help us

to prolong life for a further 50 years.

What we sentient beings really crave, though,

is a longer-lasting, more gratifying memorial.

The realization that we may simply be thrust

into the acrid ash heap of history

leaves us with the queasy sensation

we're nothing but dust whirling in a squall.

So what if we could attach our name for eternity

to a heavenly body floating in the universe --

one we could view at the nearest observatory

or even have our distant offspring pay it a call?

What if we could put our John Henry on one

of the myriad of minor planets in our solar system --

as British Columbia's Tsawout natives have done

to stake out their place in space for the long haul?

Astronomer David Balam says it took seven years

to confirm the orbit of the two-mile-wide asteroid

and have its Tsawout moniker officially approved.

But it's turning out to be a stellar fit for all.

The Tsawout people believe that, after they die,

they become twinkling, all-seeing lights in the sky.

And from this end of the telescope, at any rate,

it looks like they're beaming... and having a ball.

Law of Attraction

Humans cannot stand life
bereft of dignity.
We crave it like the sea.

A young woman sits still
in a forest dotted with deer
drawn to her by curiosity.

She senses their sprightly grace,
their nervousness.
They trust her tranquility.

They sniff the air, paw the ground.
Then, they circle around
to establish her identity.

The fawns are now so close
she can almost touch them
and their freckled beauty.

We repel others with our stress,

tenseness and anxiety.

We attract them with serenity.

Humans cannot stand life

bereft of harmony.

We crave it like a baby.

Wholesome Rest

When I lie dying on my bed,

what thoughts will enter my head?

What will I recall most

before I give up the ghost?

Will it be a fine Christmas meal

or my very first automobile?

Will it be a white-sand beach

or a lusciously ripe peach?

Will it be the perfect goal I scored

or the mysterious canyon I explored?

Will it be the stock that might've made me rich

or that miracle baseball pitch?

Will it be a row of Rocky Mountain peaks

or a set of love-making techniques?

Or will my brain be so full of clutter

that it will simply fizzle and sputter?

What did my parents think

when they were near the brink?

Or were they so sick and lethargic

that not thinking was cathartic.

While I lie dying on my bed,

I hope that I won't regret

those chances I overlooked

or the roads I never took.

I hope I'll say goodbye

with a wink of the eye

and a pat on the back

for absorbing life's flak.

I pray for a sound enough mind

not to end it all with a futile whine --

but to realize the time is best

for a long and wholesome rest.

Fog

Scrambling along the rocky beach,
there's just enough light for the dog
to dictate where we're all going.
The rest of the inlet is shrouded in fog.

A mallard or two stirs the glassy water.
But few regular human beings are out,
just folks tired of working or shopping
enjoying a challenging walkabout.

The fog is a veritable freak of nature,
a sign our volcanic universe is smoking
like a prop from a B movie about
Armageddon preparing to roll in.

This evening, there's a vast, fluffy cloud
enveloping virtually every little thing.
But what's stunning is the soft way
it's embracing us, not hemming us in.

Across the inlet, an angry foghorn booms

as a train declares its clanky presence . . .

though how it can make any progress

at all goes way beyond common sense.

Smog is often blamed on urban pollution.

But this seaside fog is clearly serving

as a gentle reminder something out there

is far more wondrous than our imagining.

Stone-Faced

One of life's minor but persistent irritations

is when people criticize you for one thing,

when the unvarnished truth is quite the other...

when they judge you by your accent, age,

complexion, hairstyle or handshake ...

or unexpected facial expression.

For many frustration-filled years, I've been told

I look stone-faced and possibly bi-polar,

and that my apparent aversion to being all smiley

is a sign of being standoffish, anti-social

or hopelessly depressed, when it clearly

has more to do with me just being me...

which is incredible in itself, since I spent

the first two months of life in an incubator

where I acquired a few shortcomings . . .

including poor breathing, doubtful posture,

imperfect skin, troubling weight variations

and a keen desire to be left on occasion

to my own devices... which often means

not doing very much except mulling things over

in a seemingly expressionless manner.

I am sorry if this leads judgy people out there

to believe I am an inexcusably difficult person

in need of extreme mindfulness training

or powerful, mood-enhancing drugs

or multiple daily visits to the gym.

But I won't apologize for omitting to smile

when there's little or nothing to smile about,

and the best way to stare down the world's critics

is to give your weary face a well-deserved break.

Just One Thing

If you watch North American politics,
you know there's a deep divide
between those who want to shake things up
and those who prefer to let them slide.

Progressives like to think of themselves
as corporate-averse agents of change.
Conservatives view them as government sucks
bent on keeping free people enslaved.

The ideological rift becomes even more toxic
with cocksure politicians such as Donald Trump
acting like the proverbial bull in a china shop
and forcing cowed citizens to jump.

The torrid pace of technological progress
is enough to give the calmest a coronary.
It barely lets them breathe before having to
fend off another invasion of privacy.

Couple that with soaring population growth,

global warming and income inequality,

and you have a recipe for mental dysfunction

covering the spectrum of pathology.

Fear and change so often go together

like falling in soccer or fighting in hockey.

They leave folks prey to total subjugation

by the nearest cartel or monopoly.

Politicians love to scare us into their clutches,

corporations to lure us into their herd.

But, deep down, conservatives and progressives

seek just one thing: a better, happier world.

Hell's Cocktail

The latest storm over chemical weapons
during ongoing Middle East aggressions
reminds me when, as a preteenager,
I mixed two brands of toilet cleaner.

The resulting cloud of chlorine gas
caused me to collapse in a mass
of acute, agonizing trauma
and suffocating asthma.

So I understand fully the revulsion
over chlorine and other production
by a cruel Syrian government
that's numb to death and suffering.

But I wonder if the recent missile
strikes aren't simply a further signal
of childlike squabbling leading to slaughter
of a thermonuclear order.

And I question why, 100 years

from the War to End All Wars,

we in the politically-divided West

are still risking our bravest and best.

I worry facile solutions from chumps

like the Putins and the Trumps

will result in the worst destruction

our fragile world has ever known.

That's why I still lather up at night,

with lungs feeling heavy and tight,

mulling over a cocktail of chemicals

that's already creating hell for ourselves.

All it Takes

All it takes is one clueless barbarian
to hold up a whole line of traffic,
maddening thousands of motorists.

All it takes is one vicious vulgarian
to ruin an entire neighborhood,
killing the fleeting magic of home.

All it takes is one narcissistic gunman
to steal the lives of guileless children
and devastate their fragile families.

All it takes, though, is one Good Samaritan
armed with heroic determination
to defuse a dangerous altercation.

All it takes is for one selfless person
to do one kind-hearted deed daily
for hope to circulate and spread.

The world is precariously balanced

between good and evil people.

Let's make sure the good people win.

Truth About Beauty

Pride, greed, lust, envy,

wrath, sloth and gluttony.

Deadly sins scramble to kill one's soul

by plopping it in some snake-filled hole.

Yet, the most enslaving passion,

even topping the allure of fashion

or a blockbuster Hollywood movie,

is our own insatiable craving for beauty.

I'm not talking about svelte Megan Fox,

Angelina Jolie and their raven locks,

but about the wonderment we feel

when we discover a truly spiritual ideal

that dwells in forests where silence reigns

or in the vastness of the Arctic plains,

or in the power of a simple prayer

or an ancient hymn beyond compare.

Still, even pursuit of the perfectly beautiful

can become dangerously delusional,

if all we care about is absurdly artificial

and settle only for the nakedly superficial.

For beauty to have legitimate endurance,

it must be tempered by peerless prudence,

temperance, courage and justice...

and love combined with gentle robustness.

Keats said beauty is truth, truth beauty...

and to know that is your only duty.

But chasing beauty for beauty's sake

is as old and stale as news that's fake.

Nose Tweak

It's a daily routine. You lose your glasses.

You search for them everywhere...

under the bed, beside the computer, in front of the TV.

But eventually, you find them in your jacket pocket,

right under your nose.

It's the same with fame, fortune and fulfilment.

You pursue them everywhere...

at a faraway college, in a foreign city, on another continent.

But eventually, you find them in your own town or village,

right under your nose.

It's the same with spiritual healing.

You search for it everywhere...

in a cathedral, at an ashram, atop Denali.

But eventually, you find it in your own study,

right under your nose.

It's the same with love.

You chase it everywhere...

on a steamy website, during a hot vacation, even at a wedding.

But eventually, you find it in your own bedroom,

right under your nose.

It's the same with beauty.

You hunt it everywhere...

in a French chateau, at an Italian gallery, in the Utah desert.

But eventually, you find it in your own garden,

right under your nose.

It's the same with laughter.

You seek it everywhere...

on Seinfeld, in a comedy club, with your workmates.

But eventually, you find it with your own crazy children

tweaking your own nose.

Swimming Upstream

Most humans cannot stand
too much uncertainty.
We need to know the sun will rise
with little or no surprise.

Like other fearful mammals,
we prefer an airtight routine
to the freedom of not knowing
which way the wind's blowing.

The more comfortable our prison,
the less we're ready to risk
maneuvering through the rills
and heading for the hills.

We'll stubbornly reject
the call of a half-open gate,
to join the overflow lineup
for a bog-standard food plate.

Our craving to be reassured
about what must be savored
is so fierce it invariably quenches
our dwindling thirst for adventure.

We'll rubber-stamp a petty tyrant
like preening Trudeau or Trump
to avoid having to think critically
about electing a qualified leader.

Rather than putting in our thumb
and pulling out a special plum,
we're wired to being herd creatures,
marching to someone else's drum.

Our penchant for wading around
with our own circle of clowns
is habitual, tribal and incurable.
Swimming upstream is futile.

Big Data

There will come a time
not so far in the future
when everything about us
will pop up on some computer.

We'll find ourselves exposed
on various information streams
as the sum of all our choices,
the totality of our dreams.

Copied onto various hard drives
or stored via multiple servers,
all our follies will be accessible
to prying Internet surfers.

They'll know what movies we watch,
what type of meals we eat,
where we go on vacation,
with whom we like to compete.

Those who've never met us
will be only too happy to tell us
how to think, behave... and
make others jealous.

And it'll all be easy peasy,
if only we learn we can be seen
and summoned to appear
on a constantly monitored screen.

Through the Ministry of Truth
and the Ministry of Peace,
we must always adore Big Data
and the party's prime police.

We must alter incorrect names,
we must rewrite inconvenient history.
We must join a righteous cause,
we must regularly claim victory.

We must remain in the cloud,
we must never resist.
We will have no will...
we may not even exist.

Magic

I'm scurrying among the pines

beside the sagebrush,

when out of the blue

a five-point bull elk

ghosts softly into view.

It stares directly at me

with its fall nobility,

only to fade back into the ether.

I'm hurrying on the trail,

glancing at the sea,

when in the blink of an eye

a Great Blue Heron

plummets from the sky.

Flapping gracefully,

it lands lightly near me,

only to vanish into the cosmos.

Animals live in a universe

of which we have

little appreciation

or comprehension.

And moments like these

are there to tease

and tantalize humanity.

Magic is there.

It's everywhere.

But you need the flair

to be sufficiently aware

to take this shaman's dare.

So tune into a herd

from the spirit world,

and you will be ready

for a surprise visit...

or grand illusion.

Homegrown Christmas

Christmas is a time for going back home.
And home, they say, is where the heart is.
But I've been away so long I can't tell
its crumbling pillars from its sagging arches.

Aging has banished so many of the memories
that helped shape my checkered career.
Also, the passage of time itself has
transformed the certitudes of yesteryear.

That rural abbey where I was a chorister,
singing carols and battling the butcher's son,
now boasts a woman bishop and has become
a magnet for urbanites from London.

The no-frills pub I once frequented,
dispensing rough cider and cheap beer,
is being bought up by entrepreneurs
anxious to make it a gourmet cafeteria.

My current home isn't as prone to flooding

as the house where I once hand-washed the dishes.

It's far more automated, more eco-friendly

and much less prone to plumbing glitches.

However, it lacks a lot of the candlelit spirit

that made my childhood Christmases such a success.

They may have been spoiled by over-drinking,

but weren't marred by political correctness.

It's easy to feel homesick about the old home

and hard to revisit it with anything but delight.

There was something so uncomplicated

about the guilt-free lives that were our birthright.

Home is where you go when you want to

savor a cigar-clouded Yuletide without regret.

It's something you never entirely grow out of . . .

nor ever manage fully to forsake or forget.

Life Circle

The other day I looked at a picture
of my father when he was my age.
He had a stubborn, faraway look,
a sign of refusing to fully engage.

It's hard to know what he was really feeling
because he was wearing the kind of facade
that even my father-in-law's heavy hand
on his shoulder was unable to disturb.

Now, one of life's most troubling truths,
one we may never truly discover,
is how we appear to others, especially those
programmed to judge a book by its cover.

Another constant downer is wondering
how many of the features we yearn to disown
are the fault of our mother and father . . .
and how many are creatures of our own.

It's easy to blame parents for a big nose

or a yearly bout of hay fever.

It's harder to blame them for our boredom

or failure to become a high achiever.

But sometimes you have the eerie sense

that, instead of a steady upward line,

time's passage is a circle... and the same

foibles keep resurfacing like corked wine.

All I know is when I reviewed my father's photo,

I found something familiar in his stare,

something I hadn't previously recognized:

It could have been me standing there.

Deadly Genetics

Time seems to move faster the older we get
and become more and more like our parents.
It's the cycle of existence that increasingly has
us crave softer music and a blander diet.

But what if, throughout our entire life,
we not only assume our parents' stubborn
personality traits, but are genetically
scarred by their terror, torture and strife?

New York professor Rachel Yehuda claims
the trauma of Holocaust and 9/11 survivors
is handed down through the generations
like icky heirlooms and double-barreled names.

Other researchers have questioned
her findings, but the key issue remains:
Are our parents our own worst enemy
in passing on chronic angst and aggression?

Stephen Paddock, the Nevada mass murderer,

is the son of a "psychopathic" bank robber.

But is this what really drove him to engage

in a seemingly senseless massacre?

I know that, for those vices I can't condone,

I'm happy to blame my mother and father.

As for my superlative qualities, though,

I'll continue to claim them as my own.

To my Mother

My mother died several months ago
and I still get waves of sadness about it,
even though to her, at 99,
it was probably a big relief.

Born at the end of one world war
and married at the start of another,
she was nothing if not resilient,
rarely grumbling about anything.

She was never averse to hard work,
mothering three difficult children,
looking after a busy, noisy home
and constantly entertaining kith and kin.

She was a proud, generous person
who was a fusser about good manners,
a stickler for high standards,
a worrier about sound workmanship.

She also was an anxious woman

who overwhelmed most people

with her passions and opinions,

without being aware she was doing it.

She had so much excess energy

it was a great pity she never had

a business she could sink her teeth into

or a corporation she could head.

My mother, however, lived at a time

when women were expected

to devote their lives to others,

not worry about their career prospects.

For nearly 65 years of her life,

she was wedded to my father.

So she must have been quite lonely

without him during the last 15.

I can't help but think she deserved
more out of this uneven equation,
or at least more worldly recognition
for the multitude of things she did.

I also believe, if she'd been raised
in a more female-friendly era,
she might have been more at peace.
So might we who'll always miss her.

Toby

I only knew you by your eyes,

because you couldn't talk to me.

But when you barked or wagged your tail,

I was mesmerized by your energy.

You may not have been the most handsome dog,

certainly not the cutest or best behaved.

Your ability, though, to dismember huge logs

will forever in canine annals be engraved.

A muscle-bound mongrel with velvet ears,

you weighed 90 pounds in full, fighting trim.

And upon reaching your physical limits,

you panted like a stressed out steam engine.

You combined a mastiff's protectiveness

with a German pointer's love of the chase.

But despite my attempts at domestication,

you never quite got the hang of a leash.

Your need for human love was insatiable.

You pestered visitors for constant attention,

relentlessly sticking your nose into their laps

until they acknowledged a connection.

Our family had you for 10 incredible years

after you chose us at the local animal shelter.

You were always a cool adventurer and swimmer,

always a warm companion and protector.

Your massive square head and giant heart

helped mold you into a dignified beast.

Sometimes, in fact, you acted so solemnly

you didn't need a dog collar to be a priest.

Perhaps that was because, as you aged,

you developed a marked shortness of breath.

The vet said it was due to some tumor or other,

and that, at nearly 14, you were nearing death.

Your throat was rattling when we told the pet hospital

that it was high time we drove you in.

You were so weak we used towels as slings

to hoist you into the back of our machine.

Speeding along, we comforted ourselves

you were in your favorite street-watching spot.

A mile from our destination, though,

you sat up abruptly . . . then you dropped.

When we lifted you onto the hospital bed,

your eyes pierced ours and made us wince.

Your indomitable spirit left your body --

and our home has felt empty ever since.

Silk Purse

Dying is not the hard part.
Living is the difficulty.
And living with adversity
is not what we're skilled at doing
in our pain-phobic society.

There's the seizing of the back,
the tingling in the feet,
the pulsing in the knee,
the whirring in the ear,
the inability to pee.

We baby boomers are a jumble
of burgeoning infirmities,
a mass of maladies,
a breeding ground for disease.
No more, please. Please.

So give us the rose-colored glasses.

Give us the big-sky views.

Give us the gumption

to pull through long years

of rejection and revulsion.

Give us the honesty

to smile at our misfortune

and the steely ability

to relieve muscle spasms

with a modicum of dignity.

Give us the integrity

to think about others

in far greater pain.

Give us the hope and faith

to get well again.

Give us the steadfast courage

of victims of acid attacks

or other means of torture.

Save us from becoming

a bellyaching blubberer.

Give us the tenacity

of a woman in labor

or a Good Samaritan

dressing the wounds

of a half-dead man.

Living is the hard part.

Living is a tricky art.

Living is a silk purse

made from a waiting hearse.

Dying cannot make it worse.

Aerobatics

I'm unable to live in the present.
I can't live in the past.
The future hasn't happened yet.
So I'm going nowhere fast.

I'm pedaling on a treadmill.
My pulse is puttering away.
But my spirit's a dark hollow,
with little or no room for play.

I'm like the Seattle airport worker
who stole his moment in the sun
by hijacking a plane he flew
right-side up, then upside down.

I too gaze out over the horizon
and look up at the stars,
despite a heart so wounded
it's zippered together with scars.

I too yearn for the motor skills

I know I must acquire

to light the remaining fuel

to make my pistons fire.

A sound way to lead a full life

is to ditch regret and shame.

So why not perform a set of aerobatics

and pretend it's all a video game?

Tree Text

It hits you the moment you leave
the mountain parking lot,
the magnetic power of trees
and their unbending dignity.

These towering conifers
lure you into nature's cathedral,
then mesmerize you
with their brooding wizardry.

Scientists say, far from being clods,
trees are clear-headed enough
to communicate with each other
via clever underground circuitry.

They "talk" to each other
through spreading roots
across the Wood Wide Web,
a vast network of fungi.

It's an information highway

that may hum with terse texts

about insect attacks, bear scat

or trade in anything sugary.

However, I strongly suspect

giant Douglas firs and cedars

shy away from selfie hyperbole

or excessive use of emoji.

The message they do offer us

as we huff and puff among them,

appears to be one of standing tall

in an unrelenting sea of dissonancy.

It's one of gradual, evergreen growth,

intelligent grace under fire,

harmony and respect...

and, above all, stillness and serenity.

About the Author

Cambridge-educated Jon Ferry has worked as a correspondent for Reuters news agency, a columnist for the Vancouver Province newspaper and a reporter for the Toronto Globe and Mail, the Edmonton Journal and the Victoria Daily Colonist (now Times Colonist).

He's covered every kind of story from the Olson murders in British Columbia to the Mackenzie Valley Pipeline Inquiry in the Northwest Territories, the Exxon Valdez oil spill in Alaska and the drug war in Colombia.

A North Vancouver resident, Ferry is the author of the poetry book Charred Horses (Prominence Publishing) and co-author of The Olson Murders (Cameo Books).

18525879R00082

Made in the USA
San Bernardino, CA
21 December 2018